GREATEST SPORTS

SOCCER
SHOWDOWN

U.S. WOMEN'S STUNNING
1999 WORLD CUP WIN

BY BRANDON TERRELL

ILLUSTRATED BY EDUARDO GARCIA AND RED WOLF STUDIO

CONSULTANT:

BRUCE BERGLUND

PROFESSOR OF HISTORY, CALVIN COLLEGE

GRAND RAPIDS, MICHIGAN

CAPSTONE PRESS
a capstone imprint

Graphic Library is published by Capstone Press,
1710 Roe Crest Drive, North Mankato, Minnesota 56003
www.mycapstone.com

Library of Congress Cataloging-in-Publication data is available on the Library of Congress website.
ISBN 978-1-5435-4220-2 (hardcover)
ISBN 978-1-5435-4222-6 (paperback)
ISBN 978-1-5435-4224-0 (eBook PDF)

Summary: In graphic novel format, tells the dramatic story of the U.S. Women's Soccer team victory in the 1999 Women's World Cup tournament.

EDITOR
Aaron J. Sautter

ART DIRECTOR
Nathan Gassman

DESIGNER
Kyle Grenz

MEDIA RESEARCHER
Eric Gohl

PRODUCTION SPECIALIST
Katy LaVigne

Direct quotations appear in **bold italicized text** on the following pages:

Pages 5, 14, 15, 17, 19, 21–23, 26: from ESPN Films, *Nine for IX: The 99ers*, (https://www.youtube.com/watch?v=IWbKYAFF5Hw).
Page 7: from "Go for the Goal," by Mariel Margaret Hamm, CNN.com, July 14, 1999 (http://www.cnn.com/books/beginnings/9907/Go.For.Goal/).
Page 28: from "Women's World Cup Soccer Team," C-Span.org, July 19, 1999 (https://www.c-span.org/video/?150657-1/womens-world-cup-soccer-team).
Page 29: from "The Spirit of 1999 Women's World Cup Lives On," by Bill Plaschke, Los Angeles Times, July 10, 2009 (http://articles.latimes.com/2009/jul/10/sports/sp-plaschke10).

Printed and bound in the United States of America.
PA48

TABLE OF CONTENTS

Down by one point at the half, U.S. head coach Tony DiCicco and assistant coach Lauren Gregg knew the team still had a chance.

Don't let your dream end today. We can play better. We have to play better.

In the second half . . .

THWACK!

GOAL! United States! Chastain redeems herself by tying up the game!

Joy Fawcett just executed a perfect header to score the game-winning goal!

FWHUMP!

Spectacular! What a finish! The United States advances, winning 3–2 as Germany goes home.

5

July 4, 1999. Stanford, California. Semifinal match: U.S.A. vs. Brazil.

SMACK!

The U.S. Women's Soccer team lived by the creed, "We before me." The players continued that team-first strategy in the semifinal match.

Goalkeeper Briana Scurry kept Brazil from scoring any points. Then a late-game penalty sealed a 2–0 U.S. victory.

The semifinal game against Brazil became cable's most-watched soccer match in history.

Go team!

Good luck!

When the teammates arrived in Los Angeles for the final match, they were swarmed by fans.

Gone were the days of poorly attended World Cup matches, like those in 1995. The United States team was in the finals, and women's soccer was more popular than ever.

Team members, such as forward Mia Hamm, were quickly becoming celebrities.

Ms. Hamm, what do you say to all the girls watching who want to be just like you?

I am a member of a team, and I rely on the team, I defer to it and sacrifice for it, because the team, not the individual, is the ultimate champion.

The U.S. women were confident in themselves and their team. However, they were about to face their most challenging game yet . . .

THE WORLD IS WATCHING

July 10, 1999. Pasadena, California. Title match, U.S.A. vs. China.

As the U.S. team's bus drove to the stadium, soccer fans lined the street to show their support.

9

After two periods of intense play, neither team has been able to score. The game remains even at 0–0.

THUMP!

Ooh! Chastain kicks the ball away, but is nearly taken out by the defender!

We're near the end of regular play, and the score is still locked 0–0. The heat is really taking a toll on the players. They appear to be exhausted on the field.

With little time left in the game, the players are fiercely battling for control of the ball.

SMACK!

Oof!

It looks like Michelle Akers is the player down.

She goes up in a tangle with Briana Scurry and actually gets hit in the head.

It appears that Akers is telling the trainers that she's OK . . .

I'm fine! I'm fine!

But the U.S. trainer wasn't taking any chances. Michelle Akers would not return to the game.

That's a tough way to end the World Cup career of Michelle Akers.

At the end of ninety minutes, the score remains 0–0! We're going into overtime! The first team to score wins!

They are dead tired. We go after it. Let's go!

But in spite of their weariness, the Chinese players wouldn't go down without a fight. They relentlessly attacked the U.S. side of the field.

Wow! That shot slipped by U.S. goalkeeper Scurry! Thankfully, Kristine Lilly was there to knock it away!

THUMP!

The blistering heat is continuing to affect the players.

Some are suffering arm and leg cramps. They're using ice and water-soaked towels to stay cool.

They chose the player they felt could be unpredictable and handle the pressure.

Do you want to take a kick?

Chastain's answer was immediate.

Yes, of course.

Gregg had a surprise request for Chastain, though.

Then kick it with your left foot.

19

SHOWDOWN AT THE NETS

Each team took turns making penalty kicks. The ball was placed 12 yards (11 meters) from the goal line for each kick.

Luck plays a factor in this aspect of the game, just as much as players' skills.

China kicks first . . .

. . . and they score!

THWAK!

USA: 0
CHINA: 1

Team captain Carla Overbeck looks cool and casual as she prepares for the United States' first penalty kick.

China gets the ball past Scurry to score goal number two!

USA: 1
CHINA: 2

FWISH!

Not sure what Gao was thinking there. The U.S. ties it at two each!

USA: 2
CHINA: 2

WOOSH!

Each team followed with another goal. But then . . .

Save, Scurry!

THUMP!

Briana Scurry makes an amazing save against China's midfielder Liu Ying!

USA: 3
CHINA: 3

This gave the United States an advantage. They had a chance to take the lead.

22

Hamm briefly gave the U.S. the lead. But China scored another goal on their final kick to tie it up.

With the score tied at four, it all comes down to this. If the U.S. scores on their final kick, they'll win it all.

USA: 4
CHINA: 4

It's likely that Brandi Chastain didn't think she'd be taking the last kick. But she doesn't seem to be letting the pressure get to her.

GOAL!

YAAAAAAAHH!

She'd done it! After 120 grueling, hot minutes. After a series of penalty kicks. After all their hard work and trust in one another . . .

. . . the United States had won the 1999 Women's World Cup!

It's a moment I'm sure these women have been visualizing for years.

For the sport of soccer, the U.S. victory was lightning in a bottle. It was a moment that would never be forgotten.

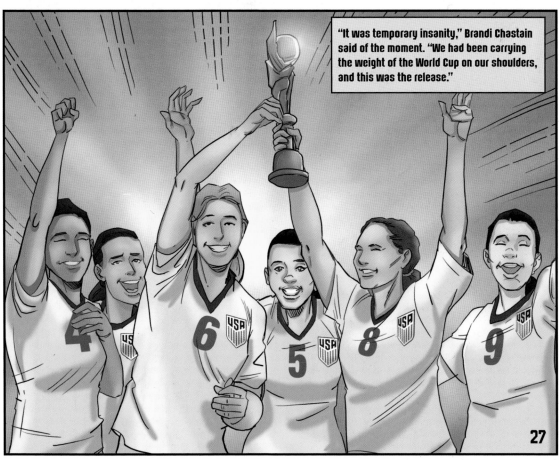

"It was temporary insanity," Brandi Chastain said of the moment. "We had been carrying the weight of the World Cup on our shoulders, and this was the release."

LASTING LEGACY

To this day, the match between the United States and China is the second highest-watched women's soccer event in history.

The players on the team, especially Mia Hamm and Brandi Chastain, became instant superstars. They went on several TV talk shows and graced the cover of sports magazines.

On July 19, 1999, the team visited the White House and was honored by President Bill Clinton.

"The women's World Cup champions . . . brought America to its feet, had us screaming our lungs out with pride and joy. They also didn't spare us the suspense. Their triumph has surely become America's triumph. We are proud of them, and we are thrilled to have them here at the White House today."

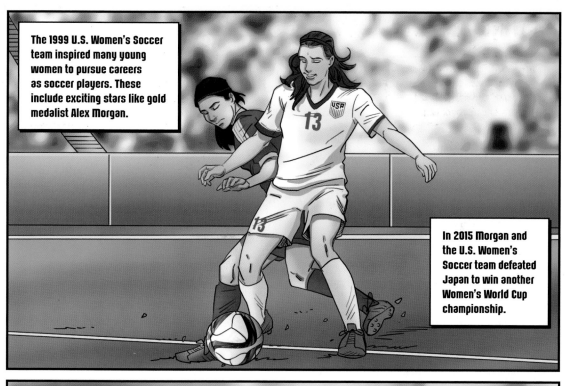

The 1999 U.S. Women's Soccer team inspired many young women to pursue careers as soccer players. These include exciting stars like gold medalist Alex Morgan.

In 2015 Morgan and the U.S. Women's Soccer team defeated Japan to win another Women's World Cup championship.

By winning the 1999 Women's World Cup, the U.S. team showed girls that with hard work and determination, their dreams could come true.

Because, as Brandi Chastain later said, *"It was about so much more than soccer."*

GLOSSARY

advantage (ad-VAN-tij)—something that is helpful or useful

creed (KREED)—a statement of basic beliefs

confident (KON-fi-duhnt)—sure of oneself

dominant (DOM-uh-nuhnt)—powerful or controlling, especially during a competition

exhibition match (ek-suh-BI-shuhn MACH)—a match played only for show and doesn't count toward team or player rankings

overtime (OH-vur-time)—an extra period played if the score is tied at the end of a game

penalty kick (PEN-uhl-tee KIK)—a free kick awarded to the offense when the defense commits a penalty

strategy (STRAT-uh-jee)—a plan to achieve a goal or win a competition

trainer (TRAY-nur)—a person who helps athletes get into condition to compete and treats injuries during a sports event

READ MORE

Hoena, Blake, with Omar Gonzalez. *Everything Soccer.* Everything Series. Washington, D.C.: National Geographic Society, 2014.

Savage, Jeff. *US Women's National Team: Soccer Champions.* Champion Soccer Clubs. Minneapolis: Lerner Publications, 2019.

Trusdell, Brian. *US Women Win the World Cup.* Greatest Events in Sports History. Minneapolis: ABDO Publishing, 2015.

CRITICAL THINKING QUESTIONS

- Star player Mia Hamm once said, ". . . the team, not the individual, is the ultimate champion." How do you think this applied to the 1999 U.S. Women's Soccer team?

- During the championship match the temperature soared to more than 100 degrees Fahrenheit (38 degrees Celcius.) Using examples from the text, explain how the heat affected the players and the game's outcome.

- Each player on the 1999 U.S. Women's Soccer team contributed to their victory. Write about a time when you helped a group or team achieve success.

INTERNET SITES

Use Facthound to find Internet sites related to this book.

Visit *www.facthound.com*

Just type in 9781543542202 and go.

 Check out projects, games and lots more at **www.capstonekids.com**

INDEX